Résumé to Z

COMMON SENSE STRATEGIES
FOR CAREER SUCCESS

JIM MOLINELLI

Palmetto Publishing Group
Charleston, SC

Résumé to Z
Copyright © 2019 by Jim Molinelli

First Edition

Printed in the United States

ISBN-13: 978-1-64111-348-9
ISBN-10: 1-64111-348-0

- TABLE OF CONTENTS -

- ABOUT ME -

As a Communication major at William Paterson College (now William Paterson University of New Jersey), I studied multiple forms of communication – film, TV, radio, and business (i.e., résumé writing and interviewing). Since then, I've written and rewritten résumés for friends, family, and numerous clients with varied career backgrounds.

When I started getting job search questions, I began to engage job seekers, recruiters, and hiring managers to increase my understanding and exposure to the job search process. I also have some unique experiences from being unemployed for much of 2009 and 2017 when I implemented strategies to secure interviews and, ultimately, employment.

With so many articles, blogs, and books that exist for every career advancement and job search topic imaginable, whose advice do you follow? (mine, of course!) My opinions are based on personal experiences, networking with those who hire, and common sense. I differ from "conventional wisdom" in some cases but, again, my opinions are rooted in common sense.

- INTRODUCTION -

Thirty-three pages, that's it. Some career-related books are 100 pages or more. I'm guessing you don't have time for that.

You need a job. The purpose of this book is to help you effectively communicate your skills and experiences and execute a successful job search – nothing more. So, I've focused only on what I feel are the essentials needed to quickly write and/or improve a résumé and navigate a successful job search.

I routinely ask recruiters and hiring managers about the résumés they receive. The most common response is "horrible." I'm confident that if you implement the recommendations in this book, your résumé will not only be less horrible, it might just be exceptional.

- THE IMPORTANCE OF YOUR RÉSUMÉ -

Some "experts" believe the résumé is either irrelevant or will soon be. Yes, some among us have gotten jobs without one by being "at the right place at the right time" or by being referred. But even in these situations a résumé was likely eventually required.

Case in point, one of my clients is a former law enforcement officer. After retirement, he set up a private investigation firm and also took personal and corporate security jobs. Recently, as a consultant, my client organized a small team to oversee security for a pharmaceutical company. After a few months of overseeing security at one building, senior management approached my client because they wanted to make him a full-time employee. They asked for his résumé; a copy was required for the file. Upon review of his résumé, they discovered his vast law enforcement and administrative experience and not only hired him, they made him Director of Security for their three US campuses.

Yes, my client worked hard to secure a job on his own, but the comprehensive résumé I prepared created an opportunity to greatly improve his employment status. Results may vary, of course.

* Some seasoned professionals think they should remove some work experiences, so as to not appear overqualified. I understand the temptation. My law enforcement client suggested the same. Instead, I documented his entire 30+ years of experience on a little over one page. How? Keep reading.

- STICK TO ONE PAGE -

I'm a big believer in the one-page résumé. Business cards and résumés serve different purposes but there's a common thread – both should contain just enough information to generate further interest and/or discussion. Yes, a résumé should be thorough and descriptive but not a novel. Think about important aspects of your career and document them with short bursts of detail that don't overwhelm the reader but adequately communicate your skills and experiences. Besides, readers likely won't make it through one page, let alone a two- or three-page résumé.

Of course, reducing a two- or three-page résumé to one page is a challenge – but not impossible. I continue to do this for clients, and each has received very positive feedback. HOW exactly do I accomplish this? In addition to retaining only the more important highlights, I look for ways to better communicate the message.

- GAPS IN YOUR RÉSUMÉ -

If you've ever been fired or laid off, you likely have a gap in your résumé. Because of and since the economic meltdown of late 2008, gaps of 4-6 months or more seem to be more prevalent and understandable. If you had a significant gap before then, most potential employers likely won't care, but be ready to provide an explanation. I think some worry that if you disappeared from the workforce for an extended period, you might disappear again.

There's no need to address gaps on your résumé, even if you're currently in one now. The recruiter or hiring manager will almost certainly ask about it. If you explain the circumstances and communicate that it took you a few to several months to land another job (if this is the reason), that should be fine because that's how long it takes to land a job in many cases.

Some gaps are longer than 4-6 months. How do you explain a gap of several years to either raise a child, care for a sick family member, or battle your own illness? A gap of this length within the past 10-12 years probably deserves a mention on your résumé. Adding a simple statement where your gap is should be sufficient.

"During this period, I focused on..." raising my three children, caring for my elderly mother, battling cancer, etc.

- ONE VERSION OF YOUR RÉSUMÉ -

Some experts recommend having multiple versions of a résumé. For special situations and circumstances, sure, I get it. For example, perhaps you're an engineer, have a catering business on the side, and are looking to change careers. Your second résumé will still include your engineering career but will also include your catering experiences. Otherwise, I recommend one that contains your complete work history and experiences. What if (unbeknownst to you) you're one of the last three candidates being considered for a job. If you have the experiences the other two have and then some, perhaps you're the one who gets hired. Or maybe you're the first to be eliminated because you're perceived to be overqualified. Or perhaps your additional experiences open doors to jobs at a higher level. You will never know.

In the section titled "Job Postings and You" (keep reading), I mention two reasons for not tailoring your résumé. For these same reasons, I would advise against multiple versions. You can rack your brain trying to figure out what to add and/or remove from your résumé or just focus on telling your story as thoroughly yet succinctly as possible.

- RÉSUMÉ OVERVIEW -

Before diving into the various components, here are a few words about the style and look of your résumé. There is no right or wrong, but after reviewing hundreds of résumés, I have strong opinions about what looks the most clean and professional.

- Your name can be one font size larger than rest of the document but otherwise use the same font size and style: 10.5, 11, or even 12, and I recommend Times New Roman throughout.
- Don't overuse bolding, underlining, or italics.
- Some abbreviations are acceptable and their use is recommended (EKG, 'Dec' for December, 'Apt' for Apartment, etc) but try to avoid job-specific abbreviations that most readers may not recognize.
- No need to label the phone number (i.e., "Cell")
- Margins can be from .4 or .7 (top and bottom) and .5 to .8 (on either side) – adjust accordingly.
- Include the month in your dates of service. Not doing so gives the impression of something to hide. For example, 2015 – 2016, did you work only two months or two full years?

- BUILDING YOUR RÉSUMÉ -

Here is a sample mini-résumé followed by a detailed explanation of how to write your own, section by section.

FIRST M. LAST

your-name@gmail.com
1 Street Name • City, State 10001
212-555-xxxx

Training, Development, and Operations Professional
with experience delivering Trading and Back Office training
programs to end-users with varying expertise (or no expertise)
at large institutional investment firms

WORK EXPERIENCE:

COMPANY ONE, New York, New York
Specialty Sales Associate   Oct 2014 – Present

- Engage customers to resolve complaints, understand a
  customer's wants and needs, assist with purchases, and
  increase 'attachment rates' (i.e., recommend additional
  purchases) – all to exceed department sales goals

COMPANY TWO, New York, NY   Feb 2010 – Oct 2014
Research Assistant (Aug 2011 – Oct 2014)

- Perform analysis of introduced legislation and present
  interest group positions and other findings to prepare
  members for a committee hearing or voting session

Business Development Analyst (Feb 2010 – Aug 2011)

- Re-engage 200+ potential customers a day, those who
  expressed an interest in purchasing a vehicle but didn't,
  and provided additional information and/or made
  appointments with sales professionals, as required

SKILLS:
Computer: Microsoft Office (Excel, Outlook, Word) •
QuickBooks
Language: Bilingual (English and Spanish)
Medical: Medical Terminology • Phlebotomy

CERTIFICATIONS:
XYZ HEALTH CARE INSTITUTE, Chicago, Illinois
Certified Nursing Assistant (CNA), May 2012

EDUCATION:
EXPENSIVE UNIVERSITY, New York, New York
Bachelor of Arts, Political Science, May 1999
Summa Cum Laude • GPA 3.75

- HOW TO WRITE YOUR OWN RÉSUMÉ -

• SUMMARY / INTRODUCTION

Immediately below your name and contact information, summarize your skills and introduce yourself to the reader. Here are three examples:

Training, Development, and Operations Professional with experience delivering Trading and Back Office training programs to end-users with varying expertise (or no expertise) at large institutional investment firms

Design / Production Management Professional with experience contributing to a variety of large public works projects throughout New York City and Long Island.

Bilingual Clinical Speech Language Pathologist with experience providing care to patients of all ages. Able to provide cognitive speech and language services to help patients function at their maximum potential.

Or just "brand" yourself if you don't have the space:

Training, Development, and Operations Professional
Design / Production Management Professional
Bilingual Clinical Speech Language Pathologist

Some are tempted to write an "Objective" here but a recruiter or hiring manager isn't interested in helping you meet your objective. A recruiter or hiring manager is interested in hiring the right candidate. Additionally, on average, your résumé might only receive a 45 second glance, if that. So instead of writing an objective, help the reader quickly determine if your résumé deserves more than a 45 second review.

First, what you should NOT do:

(1) Again, don't write an objective. The reader isn't interested in helping you "secure a middle management position at a Fortune 500 company."

(2) Don't bullet your intro. Reserve bullet points for the body of the document. Utilizing bullet points in too many areas might overwhelm the reader.

(3) Don't label your intro. This wastes valuable space, especially if you're trying to keep everything on one page.

(4) Don't be like everyone else. Stay away from terms like 'hard-working,' 'team-player,' 'focused,' etc. Instead, include qualities that are unique to you and/or what sets you apart from other job seekers.

(5) Don't write a book. Keep it to two or three sentences, no more than three lines. Anything longer is hard to digest for some. Other readers might just skip it.

If I introduced you to someone who was responsible for hiring, what would you say? This is basically what you want your introduction to be. Would you say you're hard-working or detail-oriented? Or would you say … you held multiple positions in the ------- industry, have experience supporting -------? Brand yourself, create a formal and concise summary of yourself.

• **WORK EXPERIENCE**

In the sample, two companies are listed. For Company Two, where my imaginary person held multiple positions with the same company, I left no space between the two jobs. Let's again assume the reader will spend 45 seconds or less reading your résumé. Some readers will start by counting the number of jobs you've held throughout your career or the last 5-10 years. Some recruiters and hiring managers view bouncing around from job to job as a bad thing. I can understand that. Keep jobs within the same company together (don't skip a space) so you don't give the appearance that you've had too many jobs in a certain period. Instead, show that you've been loyal and/or advanced within the same company.

• WRITING BETTER BULLET POINTS

Most bullet points are task-based:
- File documents
- Type briefs

SO WHAT? Plenty of others file and type, too.

According to a popular Project Management theory, ask "Why?" five times to uncover the root cause of a problem. Let's adapt a slightly different strategy for bullet points:
- WHAT did you file?
- WHEN do you file?
- WHO did you file for?
- Did you improve filing?
- S-T-**A-R** / C-**A-R** Method (**A**ction / **R**esult)

Begin your bullet points with active verbs to show action and ownership. Use the thesaurus (right-click on the word) to make sure you're using the most appropriate verb.

Here are a few concrete examples of bullet points from résumés I've written. While you're not going to answer every question in your bullet point(s), you do want to give the reader more than just the basics – show ownership or authority, reveal some knowledge of a process, convey expertise and experience, reveal an achievement, and/or add a bit of context.

- Develop and implement policies for 71 regional offices to meet mandates and generate cost savings
- Maintain the calendars of four executives, organize weekly meetings, and coordinate conferences
- Research, interview, and select travel management providers and establish and communicate new procedures to account executives
- Act as the group's subject matter expert and counsel sales professionals on documentation requirements and approval prerequisites
- Coordinate all office relocations and establish protocols for assigning offices for visiting attorneys
- Manage and process all employee outlays and vendor expenses within the firm
- Identify areas requiring development, recognize inefficient processes and practices, and implement changes and improvements

Here are some concrete examples of poorly-written bullet points.
- <u>Provide customer service</u>
- <u>Provide customer service</u> to those seeking to purchase tools, wood, furniture, and fixtures to maintain and repair residential and commercial buildings throughout the region

- (First example) This could mean anything. Don't allow the reader to assume that you check your phone all day and then occasionally ring up customer purchases

- (Second example) Don't devote too much space to describing the company and/or the services the company offers. Instead describe how YOU:

…engaged the firm's most prominent clients?

…understood client needs and made recommendations?

…researched product specifications to better respond to client inquiries?

While you want to add detail to your bullet points, make sure you're keeping most of the focus on YOU.

• PROCESS MAPPING AND BULLET POINTS

Process mapping is a workflow diagram, a visual representation of a process. Basically, once a process is "mapped," the visual can be used as a training tool or to analyze a process and then identify where process improvements are needed. In its most basic form, a map can capture a process in five steps:

- receive order / obtain product / package product / process payment / ship product
- order materials / oversee assembly / ship to stores / educate sales force / engage customers

Yes, you want to communicate your experiences and accomplishments with as much detail as possible but 10 bullet points or more (for each job) are a lot for someone to read. If you're taking too much space in describing your roles, consider adopting the process mapping strategy.

Your first bullet point can be a high-level summary of the position: "Manage all administrative activities for three facilities…" Next, don't randomly document your experience, instead think about presenting your experience as an organized, step-by-step process. Start at the beginning of your day. What do you do first? Once that activity is done, what triggers the next part of your day? Document this next activity. If your activities are part of a week- or month-long process, apply the same logic. How do you start this process? Do you first have to gather data or documentation? From whom? Then take the reader through the process, adding relevant and important details throughout.

Jobs don't always fit into a nicely-packaged five-step program, but if you want the reader to understand something that might be foreign to them, you need to break things down into manageable bullet points that are organized in an orderly fashion. You can get into complexities and elaborate on an interview.

- **"I NEED HELP SELLING MYSELF"**

When I interview clients about their work experiences (which I do before I write or rewrite their bullet points), I find myself asking most of them, "Why isn't much of what you just told me on your résumé?"

When you write your own bullet points, you already have a clear understanding of the many aspects of your job(s). The reader of your résumé won't. Try to avoid these pitfalls when writing bullet points:

- Sure, include details about your employer, but your main objective is to sell YOU (your experiences, your responsibilities, etc).
- Don't simply state that you "maintain a database," "process insurance claims," and/or "see patients," etc. Try to be more descriptive.
- Think about the things you do that have an impact.

What's impactful? I constantly ask clients why something is important. If they can validate, I'll ask them what impact it had on a process and/or outcome? It's hard to explain my process. Basically, I dig … and dig. After I've uncovered all the details that a client has in their head, I'm able to write new bullet points.

• CONTROL WHAT YOU CAN CONTROL

There's an overwhelming amount of guidance, opinion, and information to be digested when it comes to résumé writing (in this handbook alone, not to mention books and the web). My approach to résumé writing is simple: control what you can control. In other words, document your skills, expertise, and experiences, and then communicate this to the marketplace.

- You **CAN'T** know who wrote a job posting and **CAN'T** know if it's an accurate reflection of the job opening. For example, a friend gave notice on a Monday and was asked to write the job posting that would be used to hire his replacement on Tuesday. My friend wasn't motivated at all to write an updated job posting. He didn't, so the company recycled an old one.

- You **CAN'T** make your résumé stand out among 20, 50, or 100 online applicants.
- You **CAN'T** make people call you back.
- You **CAN** make sure your résumé highlights your skills, expertise, and experiences.
- You **CAN** try to get your résumé into the hands of those who are responsible for hiring … or the persons who may know those responsible for hiring.

- **BULLET POINTS FOR SEASONED PROFESSIONALS**

As previously mentioned, I'm a firm believer in the one-page résumé. The challenge, of course, is to present your lengthy job and educational history on one page.

From experience, an interviewer tends to discuss only the most recent 7-10 years of your work history, so focus on the present. Although age discrimination is real, I wouldn't remove too much of your work experience. While you might leave off your earliest jobs from 20+ years ago, you want to convey that you have a wealth of personal and professional expertise that job seekers under 30 don't have. The challenge is to get around gatekeepers (ironically, some recruiters) and communicate your value directly to hiring managers.

For those who began their career in a different field, condensing past work experiences should be an easy exercise, because much of that earlier experience is irrelevant. Even some experience within the same field is irrelevant and can be considerably downsized. Simply list your employers and then titles / dates for each. If, for example, you were a Sales Representative at several establishments, condense further, listing your title only once.

ABC INDUSTRIES CORP, Seattle, Washington
XYZ PAPER PRODUCTS INC, Chicago, Illinois
Sales Representative   May 1981 – Sep 1989

If you have an existing résumé, take out your bullet points – all of them – and reevaluate. Write four or five bullet points for the most recent position(s) you held. For older positions, summarize your skills into one or two high-level bullet points or simply list your job title for the oldest jobs.

What will these bullet points look like? They shouldn't be run-on sentences taking up three lines. Don't start with "Responsible for" since this wastes precious space. Instead, try to begin each bullet point with an active verb. If necessary, begin each with "Manage" and then go back and question yourself. Did you manage or did you… direct, oversee, orchestrate, solicit, reduce, increase, process, produce, and/or train? You should also look to strategically add tangible figures and accomplishments, if applicable. Did you (guesstimates are fine) increase productivity by 15%, reduce errors by 12%?

If you can't let go of your two- or three-page résumé, offer it up to anyone who wants to know more. Instead of ending your résumé with "References provided upon request" (some claim you shouldn't include this at all on a résumé but it's up to you), perhaps end with "A more comprehensive résumé provided upon request." I hope the reader calls you in for an interview instead.

You might find this new version to be inadequate. In reality, most will appreciate having things expertly summarized. Many readers won't make it through a one-page résumé, let alone a two- or three-pager. Like a business card, seek to grab the reader's interest and vividly reveal who you are professionally to generate that call for an interview.

• EDUCATION

The placement of your educational accolades will depend on where you are in life and how much work experience you have. If your work experience can propel you into your next job, lead with your work experience.

Recent College Graduates: I would consider placing your Education section at the top of your résumé (under the Summary / Introduction). If you have very little work experience, include a section for relevant courses and/or projects under your college / university. If you're still having a hard time filling the page, highlight your volunteer experience. This is experience, albeit unpaid.

Similarly, if you have **SKILLS** / **CERTIFICATIONS** / **LICENSES** / **TRAINING**, etc related to your field, I recommend all to appear above Education. For each, I recommend you follow this guidance:

NAME OF INSTITUTION, City, State
Name of Degree / Certification / Training, Aug 2015

LICENSES:
TEXAS DEPT OF MOTOR VEHICLES, Austin, Texas
Chauffeur License, Feb 2013

CERTIFICATIONS:
NEW JERSEY DEPT OF HEALTH, Trenton, New Jersey
Emergency Medical Technician, Dec 2015

EDUCATION:
NORTH CAROLINA STATE UNIVERSITY, Raleigh, NC
Bachelor of Science, Biology, May 1999
-or-
Classes toward **Bachelor of Arts**, Nursing, Dec 2025 (expected)

• ENDING IT

I usually cram too much into a résumé to fit "References pro-vided upon request." If you have the room, great. If not, then having your education at the bottom of your résumé is fine.

Now that your résumé is done, perform a spelling and gram-mar check and make sure you're using words properly (advise / advice, etc).

Your résumé is done. **NOW WHAT?**

- LEAVE IT ALONE! -
(your résumé, that is)

During the process, you should scrutinize (almost) every word to ensure you're communicating your experiences effectively. And sure, go back and make minor adjustments and/or additions as necessary. For example, a few recruiters asked me if I had client-facing experience. I did, so I added 'client-facing' to my résumé. After that, don't keep second guessing everything. It's time to share your masterpiece with the marketplace, so shift your focus to your job search.

- JUST KEEP GOING -

Be prepared to be frustrated and ignored. You might think you nailed the interview. You might think you're going to get an offer. And, hopefully, you're going to JUST KEEP GOING.

I've had the same optimistic thoughts, only to finally receive rejection e-mails for almost every job I've ever applied – for example, one exactly two weeks after applying (on Christmas evening!) and another 11 months later. There are so many variables involved in the hiring process. Not only are you competing with other candidates, there are plenty of reasons why a company or hiring manager hasn't hired you ... or anyone. Sometimes a candidate has already been identified, but the company is required to post the job and interview a certain number of candidates regardless. Perhaps the hiring manager is waiting (and waiting) for the perfect candidate. Budgeting will sometimes affect the hiring process – there's no longer room in the budget to hire or companies interview expecting to have room in the budget (and then don't). And sometimes the needs of the company or department change so their definition of an ideal candidate changes. Almost none of this will be communicated to you, which makes sense because nothing would get done if a company was always updating applicants (sometimes 20 or 50 for each job posting). All this is frustrating, but try to put it behind you and JUST KEEP GOING.

- JOB POSTINGS AND YOU -

Have you been told to customize your résumé? I can understand making minor adjustments, but have you been told to include significant parts of a job posting in your résumé? First, even though some experts encourage this, who has the time to do this for every job submission? If you've done a decent job detailing your skills and expertise, you should be fine. Second, do you know who wrote the job posting? Early in 2012, I had a phone interview … without tweaking my résumé! Not long into the interview I felt a disconnect. I then asked two questions based on the job posting, hoping to 'reconnect' with the interviewer. Instead of answers, I was told "that's not exactly accurate, the job doesn't require that anymore." My rejection letter (shocker) stated "The group is re-evaluating the position and job posting." This wasn't my first 'disconnect' experience, but the first time I received honest feedback about an inaccurate job posting.

At the same time, I was learning a lot about job postings. (1) Some may have been written after a resignation by the person resigning, and (2) job postings might be outdated, written years ago, but still used in a pinch. And some recruiters want you to reconcile your résumé to this? On top of that, you now must keep track of which version of your résumé you used to apply and bring that one to the interview. And which bullet points do you post on your LinkedIn profile?

Obviously, in some cases, customizing is warranted and good practice. But I would resist the urge and/or pressure to always adjust your résumé until you're convinced that doing so is wise and will improve your chances.

- APPLYING FOR JOBS VIA REFERRAL -

According to most experts, the best way to get a job is via referral - i.e., identify someone presently working at your preferred employer(s) and have them recommend you before or during the application process.

At smaller firms, your resource or connection might simply have to pass along your résumé to an internal recruiter or a hiring manager. At larger firms, there is likely a formal process. Understand the referral process BEFORE APPLYING!

My employer (résumé writing is my side business) requires employees to obtain the Job ID Number from candidates. At the careers section, I would then pull up each job description using the Job ID Number and then generate an invitation. The candidate would then receive the invitation via e-mail and should apply via the link in that e-mail. If the candidate was to apply at the careers section without utilizing my invitation, the candidate's application would simply be one of 20 or 50 (or more) applicants.

Before the application process, you first need to find jobs to apply to. Most are likely familiar with Indeed.com and perhaps SimplyHired.com. These and others are all good resources. Once you've found a job worthy of applying for, type the name of the company into the search box of LinkedIn. If any of your connections are currently employed at the company, ask to be referred. If a second connection is a current employee, ask your first connection if they could introduce or 'connect' you.

- THE IMPORTANCE OF NETWORKING -

Unfortunately, a well-written résumé doesn't guarantee a job, but you still need one. While an exceptional résumé may not always lead to interviews and job offers, a poorly written one will almost certainly sink your chances of securing them.

Even though I have a website, many have never visited because they've heard about my services directly from me at networking events and elsewhere. Let's assume you are finally ready to hire me and visit my website. If you found it to be sloppy or contain misspelled words, you might change your mind. My website and your résumé have a lot in common.

Yes, you should attend networking events, look up past colleagues, connect with recruiters, and tell friends and family you're looking for a job – AND make sure your résumé is not subpar. On the other hand, if you have a fantastic résumé and don't market it … you get the idea. Add your bullet points and other relevant information to your LinkedIn profile, have basic business cards for networking events, and be able to conduct yourself appropriately at networking opportunities and on interviews. And take down any provocative photos and content from your social media pages.

* Don't rely <u>solely</u> on recruiters / Human Resources. A former colleague learned that the summer intern assigned to her Capital

"Markets" group (a division of an Investment Bank) was chosen because HR found the word "Marketing" in the intern's résumé. This is just one example of why you need to be actively involved in your job search and effectively communicate your wants and needs. While it's not fair to paint with a broad brush, assume there are morons out there … and seek to avoid them.

- JOB FAIRS AND YOU -

A lot of organizations (colleges and universities, veteran support groups, industry groups, etc) sponsor job fairs to help job seekers secure employment. In many cases, this is the primary or only method of providing support to job seekers. What about all the prerequisite work (as detailed in this book!) that a job seeker should do before the job fair?

Most experts recommend networking with the folks representing the companies that you want to work for. Should you connect with them on LinkedIn and, when applicable, follow up if you find a job you'd like to apply for? Sure, why not? But who exactly are these people? Are they involved in the hiring process or just there to represent the company?

As a job seeker myself, I've gone to a few job fairs. At one table / booth, the company had a list of key jobs to fill. When I asked if I could talk to someone about the role, I was told to apply online. Yes, some companies will conduct on-the-spot interviews, but more will participate in job fairs only to promote themselves. At the time, I wondered why the company bothered to attend, but as I applied for one of those key jobs, I realized I wouldn't have known about the role if the company hadn't participated.

Job fairs may not be the most effective way to secure employment, but certainly attend them to network … with other job seekers! At one job fair, I had already been actively looking for employment for several weeks. When I encountered another job seeker interested in similar jobs, I asked if they knew that two other companies were trying to fill similar roles. The individual then shared some job search info with me. And this type of information sharing doesn't have to happen only at job fairs. If you happen to notice job opportunities, share them with the job seekers in your network.

- START YOUR SEARCH FOR AN INTERNSHIP ... NOW -

For most of us, the job search process is painfully slow and deliberate. It might start with playing "phone tag" with your initial contact, continues with trying to secure an interview date, and ends with waiting to receive an offer or rejection. Or, perhaps it never ends, and you receive no feedback at all.

For those who are looking to secure spring or summer internships or post-graduation jobs, the time to prepare is NOW as opposed to thinking you have plenty of time and waiting. At larger firms, because of the excessive number of applicants and internal end-of-year headcount, budget, or compensation distractions, deadlines for applying are sometimes as early as October or November. Even if you're not able to formally begin your quest because internship opportunities haven't been posted yet, you should still be focused on your résumé, LinkedIn profile, "elevator pitch," and networking, so you're able to hit the ground running.

If you're a freshman or sophomore in college, you can ignore the previous two paragraphs, right? Nope. I would start documenting your past experiences or at least think about what you might document. And perhaps throw yourself into a job, fraternity / sorority, and/or volunteer opportunity. You want to fill a résumé with some experiences and responsibilities, some basic skills to offer a prospective employer. In your junior year (Oct / Nov), start engaging the marketplace. If you can secure an internship for the summer between your junior and senior year (or even during senior year), your prospects for full-time employment upon graduating greatly improve.

- DURING YOUR INTERNSHIP -

Having been involved with the internship rotation and selection process twice throughout my career, I saw interns in action. When a "host" firm has a robust internship program (mixers, teach-ins, etc), most interns are able to take full advantage of their situation. Here are a few random thoughts for interns, in case you're not at a place that facilitates successful outcomes.

- Establish Relationships: As you become acquainted with employees of your "host" firm, connect via LinkedIn. To me, if anyone recognizes your name and/or face (add a picture to your LinkedIn profile), send them an invite.
- Grow Relationships: Ask a few employees (one at a time, one per week) if you can spend 10-15 minutes with them to discuss their career path, a project you're both working on, or just life in general. You might need to leverage these relationships one day (or even be able to help).

- Connect with Recruiters: I hope you're offered a full-time position at the end of your internship, but you should be preparing for life without one. Begin to connect with as many recruiters as possible. Some recruiters are good, some not so much. If you're not having success finding a good one (or 10), perhaps ask an employee during one of your 10-15 minute chats.

- "Blog" About It: Are you working on a special project or spending a week doing a specific job? Tell your LinkedIn connections. The more your connections know about you (post a very high-level summary toward the end of your internship, but don't reveal secure or confidential information), the better they can keep their eyes and ears open for potential job opportunities. Not everyone will be motivated to help you advance your career, but it certainly can't hurt.

- Update Your Résumé: You're not going to describe every detail of your internship, so once you have a basic understanding of what you're doing, add it to your résumé.

If you're given the opportunity to interview for a job during your internship (or if you're a seasoned professional), know that some hiring managers perform quite well when interviewing candidates. Others are either out of practice or not very good at all.

- TAKE CONTROL OF AN INTERVIEW -

While I think my performance on interviews is acceptable, I have ended some wishing I had been able to better communicate some of my past experiences. After one such interview, I evaluated the experience and thought how I could have conveyed more of "me" to the interviewer. While I identified areas of self-improvement, I also concluded that the interviewer had not done an adequate job of asking questions that facilitated discussions and/or allowed me to share more of my experience.

While I can't tell you how or when to "take control of an interview" (or strategically introduce important details of your career), I can urge you to be prepared to. Keep in mind, you're not going to be able to convey everything you want during an interview. However, if you feel the interview is coming to an end and an important topic was not covered, it might be wise to speak up.

And what if the interviewer gives you control of the interview? Are you ready to respond to the "tell me about yourself" question? Have a scripted, 60- to 90-second summary of your past experiences. I usually go back 7-10 years and work my way to the present. Yes, be scripted, but also be flexible in case the interviewer interrupts or asks you to elaborate on something you said.

Most of all, RELAX. Although formal, an interview is merely a discussion between two parties that are trying to learn more about each other. You do this all the time! At the end of the interview, perhaps ask what concerns the interviewer might have about recommending you for the position. If any concerns are unfounded, now is the time to address those concerns directly, if you're able to.

- HOW TO TAKE CONTROL OF AN INTERVIEW -

Have you ever purchased something that you didn't know a lot about? Perhaps you're not very tech savvy and bought a smartphone. If so, you likely had to interview someone during the purchase process. Do you remember how it went? Did the salesperson know the product? AND did he/she do a good job selling it? On a job interview, you are the salesperson but instead of the smartphone, YOU are the product. How well do you know this product? How prepared are you to sell its features (i.e., your skills and expertise)?

- What's the battery life? 18 hours
- Is there a camera? Yep, 20 megapixels
- How many apps can you download? 180

Do you give similar answers during job interviews, or do you try to also answer questions that aren't asked to demonstrate the value of the product (when appropriate)? An effective salesperson might explain how to preserve the battery and/or highlight a few of the more useful apps. On a job interview, are you showing your value by giving a little extra?

You can practice responding to standard HR questions (it can't hurt) or you can also (1) think of yourself as a product / service, (2) know exactly what it is you offer, and (3) periodically review your talents in your mind. Doing so will allow you to (1) easily regurgitate this vital information in an interview and (2) introduce vital "product" information that an interviewer might not know to ask about.

- COUNTERING THE 'OVERQUALIFIED' LABEL -

I was on the train thinking about interviewing. Yeah, I do that. And yes, I'm lots of fun at parties. Anyway, a pilot leaving the train at the airport station caught my eye. I thought to myself, "I wonder if anyone ever told him he was overqualified."

"You know, you won't be able to perform aerial acrobatics like you did in the Navy. We just need you to fly a 727 to West Palm Beach and back four times a week. I think we're going with another candidate, you're overqualified."

Airlines want pilots who can handle anything in case of emergency situations. Will you be viewed as overqualified or will the hiring manager / company value the added experience you have?

Because you may not know until the rejection letter that you're overqualified, be ready to communicate what separates you from less qualified and cheaper candidates. You'll likely be overlooked or rejected because of money so try to incorporate examples where your experience (1) prevented mistakes, (2) increased efficiency, and/or (3) resulted in real savings.

- VETERANS, YOU ARE HIGHLY SKILLED / TRAINED -

The US military is usually described as the most highly skilled and trained on earth. However, veterans are bombarded by various educational and governmental entities offering to provide and/or subsidize training. Which is it?

True, the "highly skilled and trained" description does not apply to every service member, but most veterans have some sort of operational, logistical, and/or technical skill. I would never discourage anyone from improving themselves, but military training might be enough. Consider career opportunities that don't require specialized training and/or that allow you to train on the job. Effectively communicate your skill and experiences with a résumé, "elevator pitch," and during interviews and see what happens.

- VETERANS IN TRANSITION -

When Veterans Day approaches, the media highlights the many programs that exist to help our vets: free meals at restaurants, tax credits to companies that hire vets, veteran-specific job fairs, and expressions of gratitude in radio and TV ads. One such expression, a USO TV ad, featured a service member in an airport terminal stopped by strangers who wanted to thank him for his service. Since I don't spend much time in airports, I began to think of ways to show my gratitude.

Over a period of several months, I had reached out to 10-12 veteran groups and offered my résumé writing and job search expertise. I even approached my Congressman. While one group offered one-on-one mentoring (I never did receive a mentee), the rest either thanked me for my efforts or were unresponsive. Although unsuccessful, I learned that veterans don't need help finding free meals or job fairs, but they DO need help translating their military experiences into plain English.

VETERANS, when you're asked by friends and family about your deployment (assuming you're asked), what do you tell them? I'm guessing you summarize your experiences and convey them in a manner that is easily understood. Do this with prospective employers! Make sure your bullet points convey expertise but can be understood by any reader. Here are a few examples:

- Oversee a group of five in providing logistical and administrative support to advance groups
- Coordinate all maintenance requirements for nine operational aircraft and provide leadership and mentoring to 30 maintenance personnel to produce cost-savings and increase efficiency
- Perform a daily inventory of all ammunition and mortar systems, take preventative measures to secure all property in advance of sand storms and weather-related events, and routinely inspect for damage
- Develop an improvement flow chart and policy program to streamline the purchase process and analyze vendor performance which simplified ordering, reduced timeline for receipt of goods by 30%, and reduced costs by 10%
- As lead internal auditor, analyze all procurement issues including processes, documentation, and supply and material costs

While the reader may not fully understand what you did (true with any résumé), effectively documenting your knowledge and experience will make it easier for a hiring manager to understand and assess you as a candidate and determine where you might fit in the organization.

- CONCLUSION -

Most careers require some sort of degree, license, and/or certification. The process of acquiring these credentials will likely focus on the particular skill-set (accounting, culinary, engineering, finance, nursing, welding, etc) and probably not résumé writing, job search techniques, and interviewing. So, if you're feeling overwhelmed by the thought of looking for a job, you're not alone.

Of course, a high level of job performance is important, but if you're not effectively communicating your job experiences to the marketplace or even your network, you're likely not going to find success. Writing / rewriting a résumé allows you to document your experiences out of the public eye. It's okay to 'mess up.' Just keep revising and editing until it's just right. And when you're performing a thorough assessment of your experiences, you're also preparing yourself to talk about them. This is why the majority of the book is devoted to résumé writing. It's the foundation for all job search activities.

You may have noticed that I left out salary negotiations (not much experience), how to answer some HR questions (sorry, I haven't thought about what type of tree I would be), and other topics. Instead, I focus on what I thought would bring the most value to a job seeker in distress. If you have a question about something in the book or something not in the book, please feel free to connect with me.

www.linkedin.com/in/jmolinelli